FAITH · VIRTUE

ST. JOHN'S SCHOOL

Crabs
by Lola Schaefer

in honor of
our grandson
William Carver ('41) WITHDRAWN

given by
Mama Bear and Papa Bear
(Mr. & Mrs. Risher Randall)

Crabs

by Lola M. Schaefer

Consulting Editor: Gail Saunders-Smith, Ph.D.

Consultant: Jody Byrum, Science Writer,
SeaWorld Education Department

Pebble Books

an imprint of Capstone Press
Mankato, Minnesota

1

Pebble Books are published by Capstone Press
818 North Willow Street, Mankato, Minnesota 56001
http://www.capstone-press.com

Library of Congress Cataloging-in-Publication Data
Schaefer, Lola M., 1950–
    Crabs/by Lola M. Schaefer.
    p. cm.—(Ocean life)
    Includes biblographical references (p. 23) and index.
    Summary: Simple text and photographs introduce the physical characteristics
and behavior of crabs.
    ISBN 0-7368-0245-2
    1. Crabs—Juvenile literature. [1. Crabs.] I. Title. II. Series: Schaefer,
Lola M., 1950–   Ocean life.
QL444.M33S35   1999
595.3'86—dc21   98-31445
                                                                          CIP
                                                                          AC

Note to Parents and Teachers

The Ocean Life series supports national science standards for units on the diversity and unity of life. The series shows that animals have features that help them live in different environments. This book describes and illustrates the parts of crabs and their behavior. The photographs support early readers in understanding the text. The repetition of words and phrases helps early readers learn new words. This book also introduces early readers to subject-specific vocabulary words, which are defined in the Words to Know section. Early readers may need assistance to read some words and to use the Table of Contents, Words to Know, Read More, Internet Sites, and Index/Word List sections of the book.

Table of Contents

Crabs live in or
near oceans.

Crabs have eight legs.

8

Crabs can run sideways.

Crabs have two claws called pincers.

Crabs hold food
with their pincers.

14

Crabs fight predators with their pincers.

Crabs have hard shells.

crab

old shell

Crabs outgrow and shed their shells.

20

Crabs grow new shells.

Words to Know

ocean—a large body of salt water; crabs can live in shallow water or deep water.

outgrow—to grow too big for something

pincer—a pinching claw; crabs hold food with pincers; some crabs use pincers to fight predators.

predator—an animal that hunts other animals; crab predators include fish, birds, and octopuses.

shed—to let something fall off; crabs shed their shells as their bodies grow; they have new shells that harden in several days.

sideways—to or from side to side

Read More

Cooper, Jason. *Crabs.* Animals without Bones. Vero Beach, Fla.: Rourke, 1996.

Kite, L. Patricia. *Down in the Sea: The Crab.* Morton Grove, Ill.: A. Whitman, 1994.

Moerbeek, Kees. *Crabs Grab!: A Pop-up Book.* New York: McClanahan Book Co., 1996.

Internet Sites

Crabs
http://ms.mathscience.k12.va.us/lessons/ocean/crab.html

Marine Crustaceans of Southern Australia
http://www.mov.vic.gov.au/crust/page1.html

Northeast Marine Life Slide Show
http://www.njscuba.com/Eco/Slideshow/index.html

Index/Word List

Word Count: 46
Early-Intervention Level: 10

Editorial Credits

Martha E. Hillman, editor; Steve Christensen, cover designer and illustrator;
    Kimberly Danger and Sheri Gosewisch, photo researchers

Photo Credits

Dembinsky Photo Assoc. Inc./Barbara Gerlach, 12
Ed Robinson/Tom Stack and Associates, 4
International Stock/Roger Markham Smith, 8
James P. Rowan, 10, 20
Jay Ireland & Georgienne Bradley, 1, 18
Marilyn Kazmers—SharkSong, 14
Photo Network/Underwater Sealife, 16
Tom Vezo/The Wildlife Collection, cover
Unicorn Stock Photos/Abbey Sea Photographs, 6